WITHDRAWN

RISKY BUSINESS

Storm Chaser

Into the Eye of a Hurricane

By

KEITH ELLIOT GREENBERG

Featuring photographs by
Scott Martin

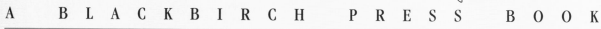

A BLACKBIRCH PRESS BOOK

WOODBRIDGE, CONNECTICUT

Special Thanks
The publisher would like to thank Jeff Hagan, Public Affairs
Officer and pilot for the NOAA, for his valuable help on this
project.

Published by Blackbirch Press, Inc.
260 Amity Road
Woodbridge, CT 06525
web site: http://www.blackbirch.com
email: staff@blackbirch.com

Printed in the United States of America

10 9 8 7 6 5 4 3 2 1

Photo Credits
Pages 10–11 (background), 22-23 (background), 26–27: ©National
Center for Atmospheric Research; pages 15, 8–9, 19, 20 (bottom),
22 (inset): Courtesy NOAA; pages 28 (top), 30: Wide World
Photos.

Library of Congress Cataloging-in-Publication Data

Greenberg, Keith Elliot.
    Storm chaser : into the eye of a hurricane / by Keith Elliot
Greenberg
       p.   cm. — (Risky business)
    Includes bibliographical references and index.
    Summary: Profiles the life of Brian Taggart, a pilot for the
National Oceanic and Atmospheric Administration, whose job
involves flying directly into dangerous storms.
    ISBN 1-56711-161-0 (lib. bdg. : alk. paper)
    1. Taggart, Brian—Juvenile literature. 2. Air pilots—United
States—Juvenile literature. 3. Storms—Research—United
States—Biography. 4. Hurricanes—Research—United States—
Biography. [1. Taggart, Brian. 2. Air pilots. 3. Storms.
4. Hurricanes.] I. Title. II. Series: Risky business. (Woodbridge,
Conn.)
TL540.T24G74   1998
551.55'2'092—dc21
[B]   96-52455
                                           CIP
                                           AC

INTRODUCTION

As he struggles to keep control of his airplane while flying through a hurricane, Brian Taggart thinks about the people on the ground. Down below, winds of more than 74 miles per hour are sweeping through towns and cities. These winds are tearing off roofs and knocking down signs. They are ripping out trees and turning items like bicycles and shopping carts into soaring missiles.

"You look down, and you see a place getting beaten up pretty badly, and you imagine the people down below holding on for dear life," says 34-year-old Brian. "It makes you feel like you're probably safer in the sky—moving with the storm—than the people getting hit on the ground."

In reality, Brian is also in a dangerous position. He is a pilot for the National Oceanic and Atmospheric Administration (NOAA). To do his job, Brian flies directly into dangerous storms and collects information about them. He calls himself a "hurricane hunter."

Brian Taggart is a special kind of airplane pilot.

5

"This isn't the safest kind of flying," Brian says. "But it is pretty unique. You're not just going from 'point A' to 'point B' like a bus driver, or a regular airline pilot. You're doing important research in a challenging environment."

Brian is an NOAA lieutenant commander. He normally works at the operations center at MacDill Air Force Base in Tampa, Florida. When he's not in the air, he spends his days planning special weather research missions.

Brian straps himself into the cockpit of his P-3 plane.

But five or six times a year, serious weather will threaten to strike an area where people live. When the bad weather is located, Brian will strap himself into his airplane's cockpit and fly straight into the storm—not once, not twice, but as many as ten times before the storm is over.

The cockpit of an NOAA plane contains many special devices for recording and analyzing storms.

Brian's 18-seat plane also carries several scientists. The data they collect during the flights may help save lives. "The whole thrust of hurricane research is predicting where a storm is going to hit," explains Jeff Hagan, an NOAA pilot and spokesperson. "When you have that information, you can evacuate people if they are in danger."

UNITED STATES

Scientists aboard the P-3 use computers and other machines to record data on the weather.

Authorities also need to know when not to evacuate citizens (remove them from a place for safety reasons). "It's hard to evacuate a city," Hagan continues. "People have to board up their homes. Businesses and schools have to close. Very sick people have to be moved out of hospitals. If you can determine that a storm isn't going to hit an area, you can save people from going through all that trouble."

Brian has been specially trained to fly in dangerous weather situations.

Many times during a hurricane, Brian's entire airplane has rocked violently. "I won't say you lose control of the airplane," he says. "But sometimes you question whether it's you or Mother Nature in charge."

Still, he insists, he doesn't allow himself to feel frightened. "You never get scared when you fly," he says. "You become concerned because there's danger up there. But we're highly trained, and we can handle most situations."

Understanding Weather: What Is a Hurricane?

A hurricane is a type of tropical cyclone. A tropical cyclone is a large storm that forms over tropical waters. Sometimes it strikes targets on land. In the Northern Hemisphere, these storms move counterclockwise. There are three types of tropical cyclones:

1. **Tropical Depression:** a swirling system of clouds and thunderstorms with maximum winds of 38 miles per hour.

2. **Tropical Storm:** a swirling system of strong thunderstorms with winds of 39 to 73 miles per hour.

3. **Hurricane:** a swirling system with winds of at least 74 miles per hour. In the western Pacific Ocean, these are called "typhoons." In the Indian Ocean, similar storms are labeled "cyclones."

Good pilots have a strong knowledge of weather patterns.

Brian learned to appreciate the rules of flight from his father, Kelly, who was also a pilot for NOAA. Unlike his son, however, Kelly Taggert's job involved making maps and charts, not researching the weather.

At Maryland's Rockville High School, Brian took an aviation course, where he

12

learned U.S. flying rules, navigation, and meteorology (the study of weather). He also took flying lessons.

After high school, Brian attended the Florida Institute of Technology. There, he continued with his aviation training. He also studied math and science, which were required for all aviation students.

"Knowing these subjects makes you a better pilot," Brian says. "If you take an airplane off the ground, you have to respect the laws of nature. Without math and science, you can't really understand the laws of nature."

After college, Brian became a flight instructor. But all his life, he'd wanted to follow his father to the NOAA.

Understanding Weather: Types of Hurricanes

According to the Saffir-Simpson Hurricane Scale—a system of measuring these kinds of storms—hurricanes can be divided into these five categories:

Category	Winds (miles per hour)
1	74-95
2	96-110
3	111-130
4	131-155
5	155 or more

13

In preparation for a mission, Brian inspects the underside of his plane.

There are only 320 members of the exclusive "NOAA Corps." It is very difficult to join. For every five people who apply, one is chosen. Brian was picked for the NOAA Corps in 1985 because he was a licensed pilot who had also studied calculus and physics in college.

Brian didn't become a hurricane hunter right away. At first, he studied the seasonal movements of animals in Alaska and the Gulf of Mexico. From his plane, he tracked groups of seals, whales, polar bears, and sea turtles. Later, like his father, Brian took aerial photographs of the U.S. coastline for maps and charts. Finally, in 1994, he was chosen to fly the Lockheed WP-3D Orion, the NOAA's largest plane. The P-3 is used to track hurricanes.

The NOAA uses its largest plane, the P-3, to track hurricanes.

Each P-3 has a
special sticker that
marks the plane's
duty in a hurricane.

There are two P-3s headquartered at Brian's base. One is called "Miss Piggy," after the muppet character on *Sesame Street*. "It's a big, wide plane," Brian points out, "kind of like a pig."

The other aircraft is named after another *Sesame Street* character, "Kermit the Frog."

18

Along with a decal of either Miss Piggy or Kermit, every P-3 has a sticker for each hurricane it has seen. In 1996, for instance, "Kermit" had 59 stickers on its side. The first was for Hurricane Bonny in 1976. The last sticker was for Hurricane Lili, which occurred 20 years later.

There are also decals for each of the countries the plane has visited, including India, Australia, Malaysia, and Greenland.

Two of the NOAA's planes are named after Sesame Street characters: "Kermit" and "Miss Piggy."

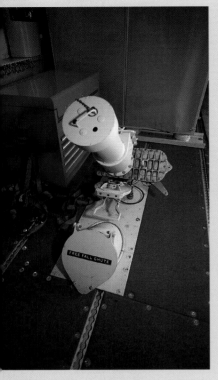

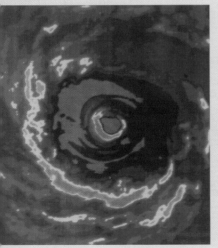

When a serious storm begins, NOAA's satellites first monitor it from high above the earth. The satellites take photos and determine the storm's general location. Then, the P-3 airplanes are needed. Once the pilot reaches the center of the storm, the scientists on board can tell how fast the disturbance is moving, and in what direction.

Because hurricanes often rock the plane, the scientists are strapped in to their work stations. They must wear headsets to communicate with each other.

An important piece of equipment is the "radome"—or radar dome—which is connected to the underside of the plane. Another radome is placed on the tail, and another on the nose. The radar helps

Opposite top: Storm-monitoring devices are released to the outside through this hatch, called a free-fall chute.
Opposite bottom: Satellite images of storms are often the first view of dangerous weather.
Right: Brian stands in front of the nose of an airplane equipped with radar and a long antenna.

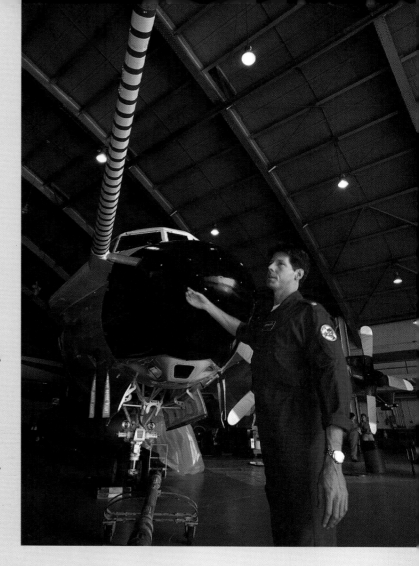

the scientists figure out the strength of the storm. It also helps the pilot find patches of sky where the rain is less severe. It is through these patches that Brian tries to fly, as he guides his plane to the center of the storm.

Though there are bands
of dangerous weather
swirling around the
storm's center, the "eye"
is often perfectly calm.

As he approaches a storm, Brian is filled with wonder and excitement. "It's really a beautiful site," he says. "From 200 miles away, you can see this white haze of clouds. And you tell yourself, 'This is it. We're going into a hurricane.'"

At this point, Brian sees the "feeder bands." These are rings of thundering weather that circle around the center— or "eye"—of the storm. Unlike the feeder bands, the eye of the storm is calm. It is so calm, it is often eerie. This area, usually between 2 and 20 miles wide, is often marked by clear, blue sky. The feeder bands that surround the eye of the storm can be dangerous. The worst is the "eye wall," the wall of bad weather surrounding the storm's eye.

Understanding Weather: How Hurricanes Are Named

Naming hurricanes is very useful. It helps weather scientists, called meterologists, keep track of storms. When there is more than one storm in an area, using names is especially helpful.

An Australian meterologist named Clement Wragge was the first to name hurricanes after women. He also decided to name them in alphabetical order, beginning with A and working to Z as the year went on.

Starting in 1979, both men's and women's names were given to hurricanes in alternating fashion.

Today, the World Meterological Organization chooses the official names for hurricanes around the world. Here are the official names that have been chosen for storms that occur between 1998 and 2000:

1998	1999	2000
Alex	Arlene	Alberto
Bonnie	Bret	Beryl
Charley	Cindy	Chris
Danielle	Dennis	Debby
Earl	Emily	Ernesto
Frances	Floyd	Florence
Georges	Gert	Gordon
Hermine	Harvey	Helene
Ivan	Irene	Isaac
Jeanne	Jose	Joyce
Karl	Katrina	Keith
Lisa	Lenny	Leslie
Mitch	Maria	Michael
Nicole	Nate	Nadine
Otto	Ophelia	Oscar
Paula	Philippe	Patty
Richard	Rita	Rafael
Shary	Stan	Sandy
Tomas	Tammy	Tony
Virginia	Vince	Valerie
Walter	Wilma	William

Winds in the eye wall frequently blow at more than 100 miles per hour. "The more intense the weather, the harder it is on your plane," Brian says. "And if you damage your plane, you put yourself in danger. Mother Nature has brought many airplanes down in situations where pilots didn't fully understand the weather."

The strength of the weather can vary from one feeder band to another. These quick changes often make flying through a storm a strange experience for a pilot. There are moments when the plane glides smoothly. Then, suddenly, the aircraft rocks violently.

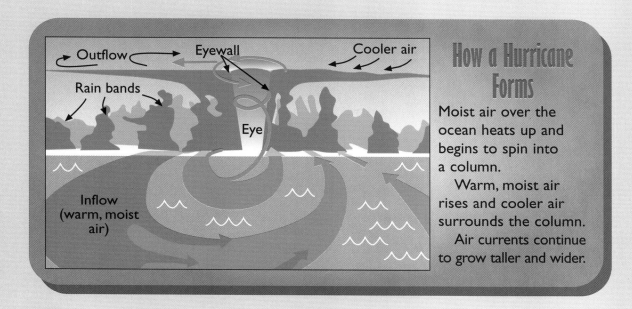

Outflow   Eyewall   Cooler air

Rain bands

Eye

Inflow
(warm, moist
air)

How a Hurricane Forms

Moist air over the ocean heats up and begins to spin into a column.

Warm, moist air rises and cooler air surrounds the column.

Air currents continue to grow taller and wider.

"Sometimes, you can't even read your instruments because they're shaking so much," Brian says. "And the rain smacking against your windshield is so loud, you can't hear anything else."

Brian's airplane has been hit by lightning a few times. "It's hard to describe what that feels like," he says. "You're looking through the windshield, and watching a lightning bolt snapping and cracking against the nose of the plane. And lightning can blow out equipment, or blast a hole into the plane. All you can do is keep control of the aircraft, and hope that things don't get any worse."

 **Brian and his fellow pilots always keep in mind the awesome power of nature.**

After flying through the eye wall, Brian enters the eye of the storm. His goal now is to find the storm's point of origin, one small spot where there is no wind at all. "When you find this point, it helps you measure the storm's direction and speed," Brian says.

27

Above: Hurricane Hugo caused billions of dollars in damage when it hit land in 1989.
Right: Brian walks through the cabin area of his P-3.

Once the plane is in the eye of the storm, everything is calm. The pilot and the scientists on board stand up, stretch their legs, and fix themselves sandwiches and drinks in the airplane's "galley," or kitchen. "This is the time to relax," Brian says, "because soon you're going to have to exit the storm, and pass through all that shaking again."

Understanding Weather: A Brief Hurricane History

1. **Camille** (1969): 27 inches of rain fell in Virginia. The hurricane caused a great deal of flooding and property damage.

2. **Agnes** (1972): caused 15 tornadoes in Florida and two in Georgia. The storm created floods from New York to North Carolina.

3. **Hugo** (1989): Hurricanes usually form at sea, and then weaken as they hit land. But Hugo was still going strong 175 miles from the ocean, causing winds to move as fast as 100 miles per hour in Charlotte, North Carolina.

4. **Andrew** (1992): winds in south Florida were at least 175 miles per hour. This hurricane caused an estimated $25 billion in damage.

A Florida resident sits among the wreckage of his home after Hurricane Andrew hit in 1992.

Many times, after a storm has passed, Brian accompanies rescue teams. With others, he helps people whose homes were wrecked by a hurricane. "It's an eerie feeling," he says. "Houses are destroyed. Trees are lying on their sides. Electric poles and power lines are on the ground. It looks just like a war zone. The only thing missing is the shooting."

It's during these times that Brian realizes the true importance of his job. "It's not easy flying through hurricanes," he says. "But when you're back on the ground, with your plane and crew safe, you think about how the information you collected is going to help people, and maybe save some lives. That's when you feel really satisfied."

Brian's job in the air is dangerous, but his work helps to protect many people from danger on the ground.

FOR MORE INFORMATION

Books

Greenberg, Keith. *Hurricanes and Tornadoes*. New York: Twenty-First Century Books, 1994.

Kahl, Jonathan D. *Storm Warning: The Power of Tornadoes and Hurricanes*. Minneapolis, MN: Lerner Group, 1993.

Lampton, Christopher. *Hurricane*. Brookfield, CT: Millbrook Press, 1991.

Web Sites

http://www.sun-sentinel.com/storm/
Provides information on a variety of weather-related subjects, including statistics and charts on hurricanes, and a virtual tour of a Lockheed WP-3D Orion airplane.

http://www.nhc.noaa.gov/
For the National Hurricane Center's Tropical Prediction Center. Information on past hurricanes and tropical cyclones with graphics.

http://205.156.54.206/
The National Weather Service's homepage. Information about current weather patterns, climate statistics, history, and discussion of various weather topics.

INDEX

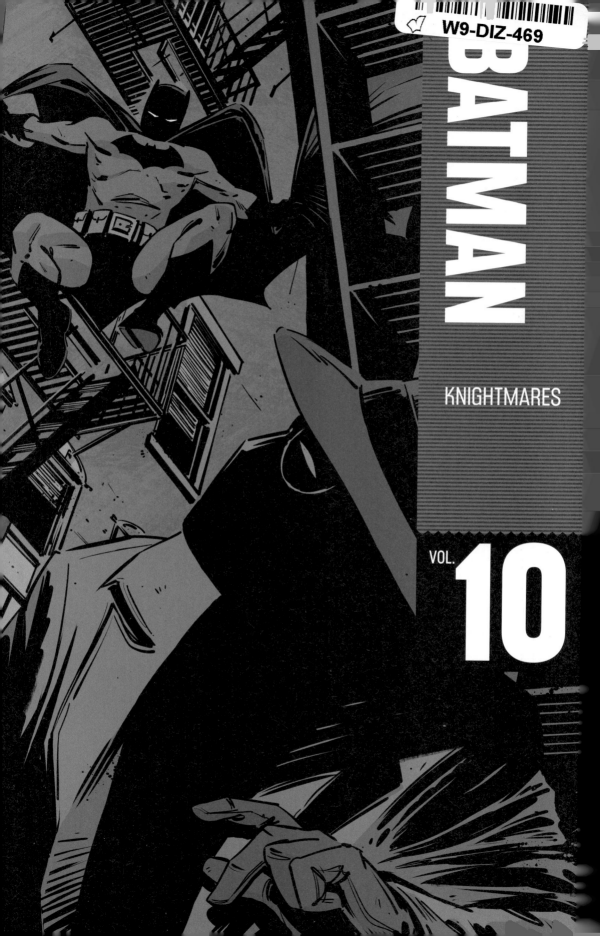

BATMAN

KNIGHTMARES

VOL. **10**

BATMAN
KNIGHTMARES

writer
TOM KING

artists
TRAVIS MOORE
MITCH GERADS
MIKEL JANÍN
JORGE FORNES
LEE WEEKS
AMANDA CONNER
DAN PANOSIAN
JOHN TIMMS
YANICK PAQUETTE

colorists
TAMRA BONVILLAIN
MITCH GERADS
JORDIE BELLAIRE
DAVE STEWART
LOVERN KINDZIERSKI
PAUL MOUNTS
JOHN TIMMS
NATHAN FAIRBAIRN

letterer
CLAYTON COWLES

collection cover artist
MIKEL JANÍN

BATMAN created by BOB KANE with BILL FINGER
SUPERMAN created by JERRY SIEGEL and JOE SHUSTER
By special arrangement with the Jerry Siegel family

VOL. **10**

JAMIE S. RICH Editor – Original Series
BRITTANY HOLZHERR Associate Editor – Original Series
JEB WOODARD Group Editor – Collected Editions
ROBIN WILDMAN Editor – Collected Edition
STEVE COOK Design Director – Books
LOUIS PRANDI Publication Design
ERIN VANOVER Publication Production

BOB HARRAS Senior VP – Editor-in-Chief, DC Comics
PAT McCALLUM Executive Editor, DC Comics

DAN DiDIO Publisher
JIM LEE Publisher & Chief Creative Officer
BOBBIE CHASE VP – New Publishing Initiatives & Talent Development
DON FALLETTI VP – Manufacturing Operations & Workflow Management
LAWRENCE GANEM VP – Talent Services
ALISON GILL Senior VP – Manufacturing & Operations
HANK KANALZ Senior VP – Publishing Strategy & Support Services
DAN MIRON VP – Publishing Operations
NICK J. NAPOLITANO VP – Manufacturing Administration & Design
NANCY SPEARS VP – Sales
MICHELE R. WELLS VP & Executive Editor, Young Reader

BATMAN VOL. 10: KNIGHTMARES

DC Comics, 2900 West Alameda Ave., Burbank, CA 91505
Printed by LSC Communications, Owensville, MO, USA. 8/9/19. First Printing.
ISBN: 978-1-77950-158-5

Library of Congress Cataloging-in-Publication Data is available.

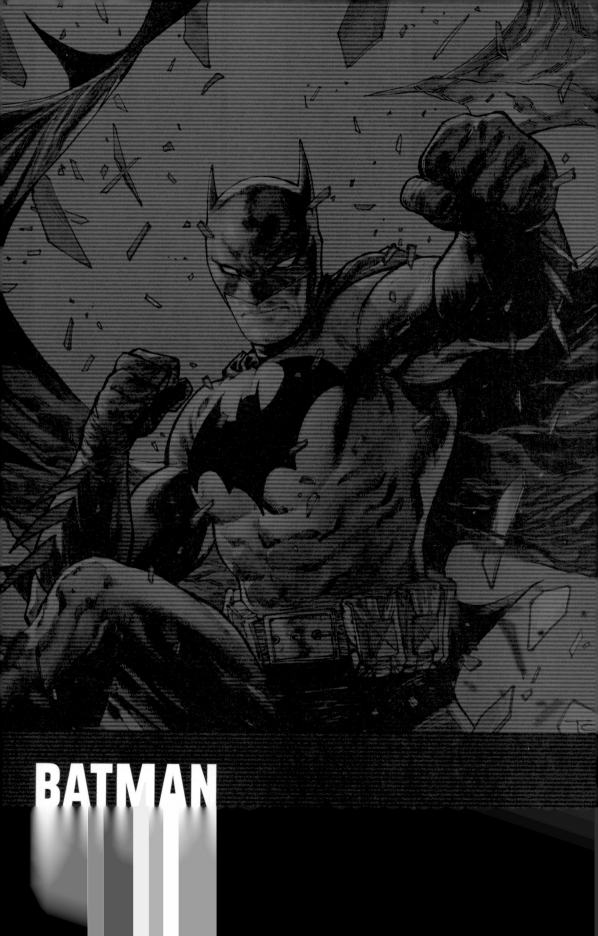

LAST FRIDAY! BALD GUY! SIX FEET TALL!

DIDN'T GIVE HIS NAME! SAID HE GOT MY NAME FROM *FRANK GIALLA!*

GIALLA'S MADE! I GAVE HIM WHATEVER HE WANTED! A THOUSAND DOLLARS!

THANK YOU.

OKAY, TH-THAT'S ALL I HAVE, I GAVE Y-YOU WHATEVER I HAD, I SWEAR, HONEST.

AND N-NOW YOU W-WON'T DO IT, RIGHT? YOU PROMISE? S-SAY YOU WON'T DO IT.

S-SAY YOU WON'T D-DROP ME.

I WON'T DROP YOU.

NOOO!

AAAAAAAA!!!

BBNGG

CHGCHGCHGCHGCHG

CHOOOOO

CHOOOOOO

BMMPP

CHGCHGCHGCHG

BRUCE, WOULD YOU PLEASE READ THE OPENING PASSAGE OUT LOUD?

I THINK FITZGERALD'S LANGUAGE HERE IS PARTICULARLY STRIKING.

Y-YES, MR. WOOD.

"OF COURSE, ALL LIFE IS A PROCESS OF BREAKING DOWN...

"...BUT THE BLOWS THAT DO THE DRAMATIC SIDE OF THE WORK--

"--THE BIG SUDDEN BLOWS THAT COME, OR SEEM TO COME, FROM OUTSIDE--

"THE ONES YOU REMEMBER AND BLAME THINGS ON AND...

"...IN MOMENTS OF WEAKNESS, TELL YOUR FRIENDS ABOUT...

"...DON'T SHOW THEIR EFFECT ALL AT ONCE."

"THERE IS ANOTHER SORT OF BLOW THAT COMES FROM WITHIN..."

"...THAT YOU DON'T FEEL UNTIL IT'S TOO LATE TO DO ANYTHING ABOUT IT..."

"UNTIL YOU REALIZE..."

"WITH FINALITY..."

"...THAT IN SOME REGARD YOU WILL NEVER BE AS GOOD A MAN AGAIN."

"THE FIRST SORT OF BREAKAGE SEEMS TO HAPPEN QUICK--

"THE SECOND KIND HAPPENS ALMOST WITHOUT YOUR KNOWING IT...

"...BUT IS REALIZED SUDDENLY INDEED."

HEY, KID.

LONG TIME...

LOOK, I'M NOT TOO GOOD WITH ALL THE WORDS.

BUT I DO AT LEAST WANT TO TRY TO, Y'KNOW, SAY I'M SORRY.

I GET THAT'S NOT ANYTHING TO YOU.

BUT I DIDN'T MEAN ANYTHING.

I DIDN'T GET ANYTHING FROM IT.

IT WAS JUST...

AAAAAA!!!

SLICE

AAAAAA!!!

AAAAAA!!!

AAAAAA!!!

AAAAAA!!!

AAAAAA!!!

AAAAAAA!!!

AAAAAA!!!

AAAAAA!!!

"WHAT IS THIS, THE SIXTH?"
"SEVENTH. THE SAME EVERY TIME. WHOEVER IT IS. 'HE KILLED MY PARENTS.'"
"LORD."
"HE HAS RESOURCES. BRIBES GUARDS, INMATES. WE THINK HE'S GETTING HELP FROM THE ESCAPED BUTLER, THIS *TAYLOR.*"
"IT'S TOO MANY DEAD. WE CAN'T HAVE HIM HERE. IT'S OVER."
"ARKHAM?"
"HE'S YOUNG. BUT THEY'RE THE ONLY...AT LEAST IT WOULDN'T BE OUR PROBLEM."
"THEY DESERVE IT. LET THEM DEAL WITH MATTHEW."
"NO, NO, DIDN'T YOU HEAR?"
"WHAT?"
"LET THEM DEAL WITH *MASTER BRUCE.*"
MOTHER... FATHER...
I LOVE YOU.
I MISS YOU SO.
DC COMICS PRESENTS
KNIGHTMARES, PART 1
"Suddenly Indeed"
TOM KING WRITER TRAVIS MOORE ARTIST TAMRA BONVILLAIN COLOR ARTIS
CLAYTON COWLES LETTERER TONY S. DANIEL & TOMEU MOREY COVER
BRITTANY HOLZHERR ASSOCIATE EDITOR JAMIE S. RICH EDITOR

BATMAN
#62

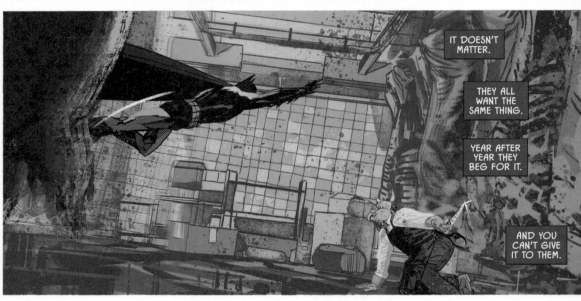

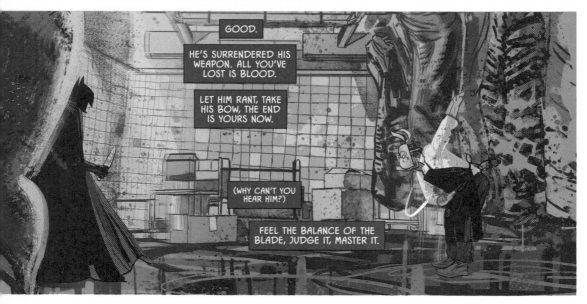

THROW IT.

PERFECT.

HE'S BROKEN, BY HIS OWN WEAPON, BROKEN.

ON THE GROUND, LAUGHING. THEY ALL LIKE TO LAUGH. PYG LOVES TO LAUGH.

(LITTLE PIG, LITTLE PIG, LET ME IN.)

EVERYTHING'S A JOKE, EVERYONE'S THE JOKER.

EVERYONE BUT *YOU.*

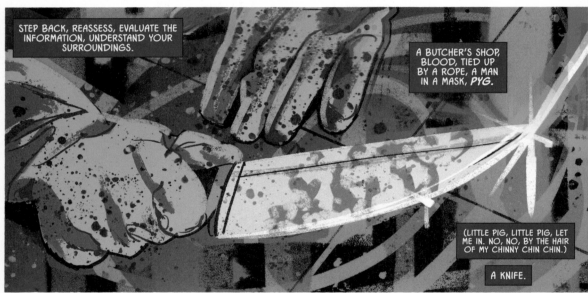

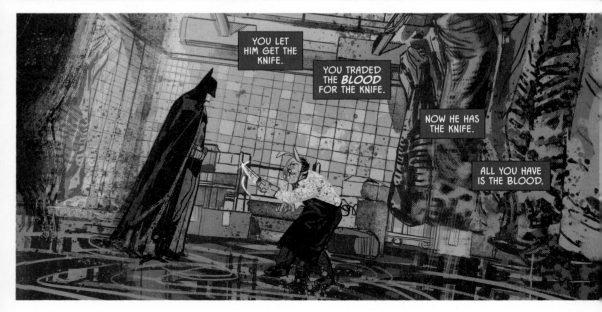

NO!

FORGET BANE! LOOK. LOOK HERE. *HERE* IS YOUR FIGHT.

THROW SOMETHING, BATARANGS, TWO BATARANGS, TWIST YOUR FINGERS, LET THEM SPIN.

SHUT HIM UP! ENOUGH TALKING!

YOU'RE WEAK, BUT YOU CAN THROW.

(WHY DID HE LEAVE YOU WITH WEAPONS?)

BUT BANE...

YOU WERE IN THE CAVE. ALFRED SAID IT WAS FATHER.

YOU TURNED. YOU SAW...

HIS EYES WERE *RED.*

HOW DID YOU GET HERE?

HOW DO YOU GET OUT?

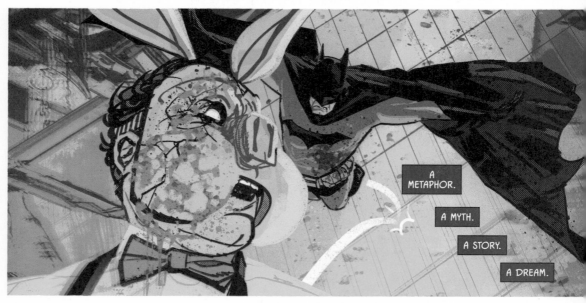

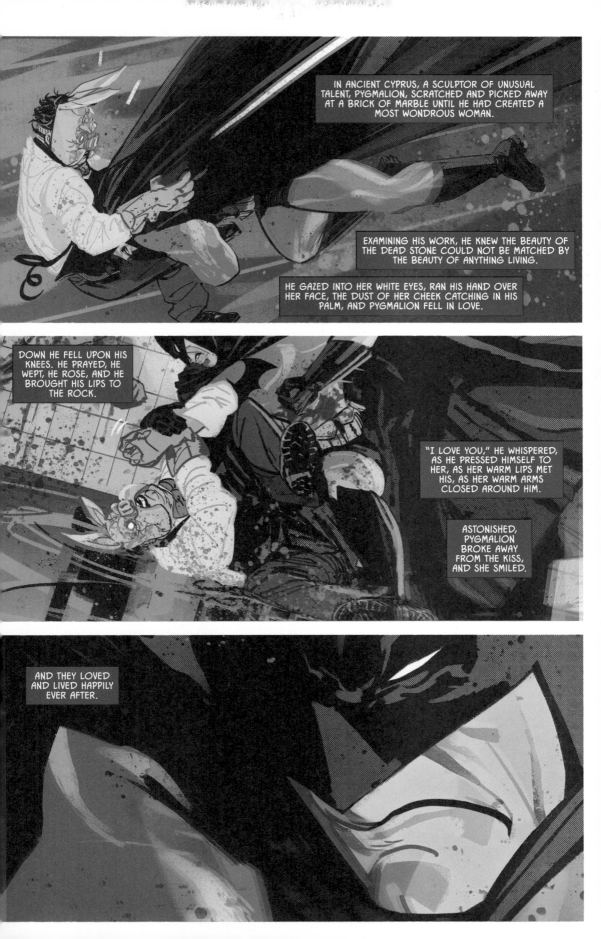

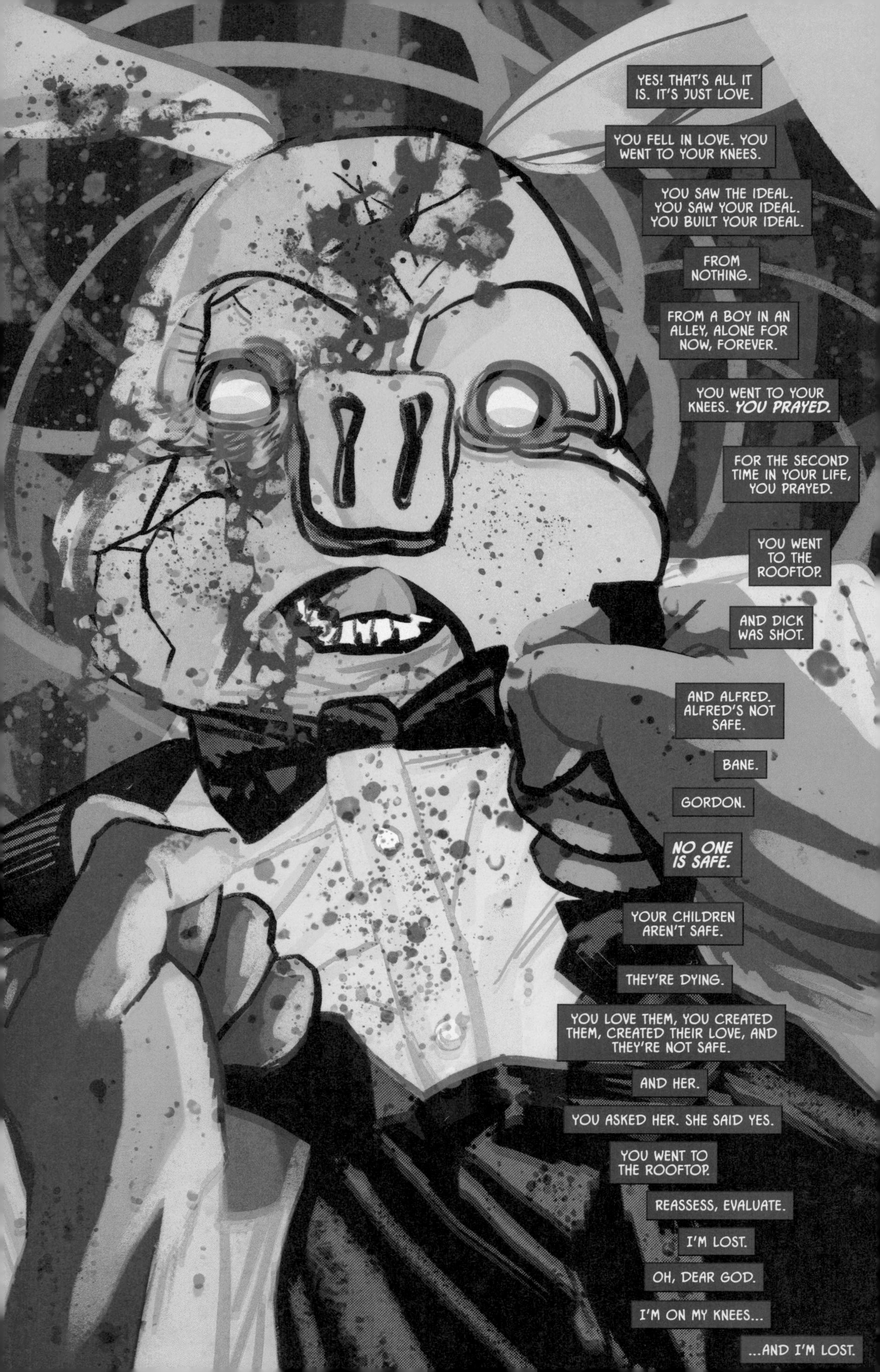
YES! THAT'S ALL IT IS. IT'S JUST LOVE.
YOU FELL IN LOVE. YOU WENT TO YOUR KNEES.
YOU SAW THE IDEAL. YOU SAW YOUR IDEAL. YOU BUILT YOUR IDEAL.
FROM NOTHING.
FROM A BOY IN AN ALLEY, ALONE FOR NOW, FOREVER.
YOU WENT TO YOUR KNEES. ***YOU PRAYED.***
FOR THE SECOND TIME IN YOUR LIFE, YOU PRAYED.
YOU WENT TO THE ROOFTOP.
AND DICK WAS SHOT.
AND ALFRED. ALFRED'S NOT SAFE.
BANE.
GORDON.
NO ONE IS SAFE.
YOUR CHILDREN AREN'T SAFE.
THEY'RE DYING.
YOU LOVE THEM, YOU CREATED THEM, CREATED THEIR LOVE, AND THEY'RE NOT SAFE.
AND HER.
YOU ASKED HER. SHE SAID YES.
YOU WENT TO THE ROOFTOP.
REASSESS, EVALUATE.
I'M LOST.
OH, DEAR GOD.
I'M ON MY KNEES...
...AND I'M LOST.

THE SMELL.

THE RANCID CORPSES OF ALL THE PIGS.

BRED.

SLAUGHTERED.

HANGING.

WAITING.

ASK HIM.

OPEN YOUR EYES.

OPEN YOUR DAMN EYES!

ALL THE PIGS ON ALL THE HOOKS.

EVERYWHERE YOU LOOK, EVERYTHING YOU SEE, EVERYTHING YOU ARE.

BRED. SLAUGHTERED. HANGING. WAITING.

ASK HIM.

ASK HIM!

KNIGHTMARES, PART 2
"Lost"

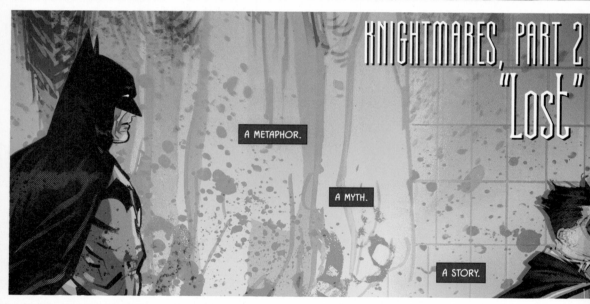

TOM KING WRITER
MITCH GERADS ARTIST AND COVER
CLAYTON COWLES LETTERER
BRITTANY HOLZHERR ASSOCIATE EDITOR   JAMIE S. RICH EDITOR

BATMAN
#63

IF WE WAIT ANOTHER HOUR...

...I'M GONNA NEED ANOTHER DRINK.

OR FOUR.

PERHAPS SOMETHING...

NO.

MASTER BRUCE?

SIR?

BAT.

I WAS RUNNING. I DON'T KNOW HOW OLD I WAS. I'D HAD THE DREAM BEFORE.

AND MUM WAS RUNNING WITH ME. ALONGSIDE ME. I THINK WE WERE GOING TO A WEDDING. BEST I CAN REMEMBER.

THERE WERE COLORS IN IT. ALL THESE SHADES OF RED THAT YOU DON'T SEE ANYWHERE IN LIFE. THAT YOU KNOW YOU'LL NEVER SEE AGAIN SO YOU THINK TO PAUSE AND LOOK AT THEM, AND BY THE TIME YOU LOOK, THEY'VE GONE BLUE, EVERYTHING LOOKS BLUE AND SOMEONE'S YANKING AT YOU TO KEEP GOING, AND IT'S YOUR MUM, AND YOU'RE LATE.

AS WE WENT, SHE FELL HARD. I DON'T KNOW WHY. I THINK SHE TRIPPED. MAYBE SHE DIDN'T. WHO'S TO SAY?

I HELPED HER UP. SHE WAS LAUGHING. THERE WAS BLOOD BETWEEN HER TEETH.

WE KEPT RUNNING. NOT IN ONE PLACE. SOMETIMES THE ROAD, SOMETIMES THE SKY.

AND SHE FELL AGAIN. I ASKED HER WHAT WAS WRONG. SHE SAID IT WAS NOTHING AND I HELPED HER UP, BUT SHE WAS LIMPING NOW. SHE WAS HURT.

('COURSE, ODD THING IS MUM DIED WHEN I WAS BORN. I ENTERED LIFE, SAW THE LIGHT, CRIED OUT BECAUSE THE LIGHT'S TOO DAMN BRIGHT, ISN'T IT? WELL, MUM HEARD THAT AND WASN'T HAVING IT, AND SHE PASSED OFF AS QUICKLY AS SHE COULD MANAGE.)

ANYHOW, MUM AND I WERE RUNNING AND SHE FELL AGAIN, AND AGAIN, AND THERE WERE BRUISES UP HER ARM AND HER BACK, AND I KEPT HELPING HER, BUT WE WERE LATE.

FINALLY, SHE SAID TO GO ON. SHE WAS STILL LAUGHING. STILL HAD BLOOD BETWEEN HER TEETH.

SHE LOOKED AT ME AND I SAW MY DAUGHTER IN HER, THOUGH I KNEW I'D NEVER HAVE A DAUGHTER, AND SHE TOLD ME TO GO.

GET THERE, MY BOY.

AND I LEFT HER ON T ROAD OR THE SKY.

AT THE END OF THIS...

SHE'S GOING TO DIE.

I'LL PROTECT HER.

IT'S GOT NOTHING TO DO WITH YOU.

EXCEPT FOR THE FACT THAT IT'S GOT *EVERYTHING* TO DO WITH YOU.

YOU WORRY TOO MUCH, JOHN.

YEAH.

MAYBE.

I DON'T SEE HOW ANY OF THIS IS YOUR BUSINESS.

IT'S *NOT*, FRIEND.

AND I'M NOT SAYING IT IS.

JUST TRYING TO HELP.

I DON'T NEED YOUR HELP.

THE CLUE TWO-FACE LEFT INSIDE THE DEAD TWINS.

THERE WERE *TWO* POSSIBLE ANSWERS. *TWO* POSSIBLE LOCATIONS.

FOOTBALL KNIGHTS STADIUM OR THE BASEBALL KNIGHTS STADIUM.

I'M COVERING ONE. SHE'S COVERING THE OTHER.

ALONE?

SHE'S GOOD.

SHE DOESN'T NEED ME.

SHE'S FINE.

I'M SURE. BUT MIND IF I ASK A QUESTION?

WHY DID THE JAIL LET *MASTER BRUCE* KILL THOSE CHILDREN?

THEY COULDN'T HAVE DONE ANYTHING TO STOP THAT?

AND FOR THAT MATTER, IN THE MEAT LOCKER...

HOW'D IT TAKE YOU SO LONG TO FIGURE OUT PYG WAS YOUR BOY?

AIN'T YOU THE WORLD'S GREATEST DETECTIVE?

SHE'S FINE.

IF WE CAN'T FIX THE CLOCK, CAN WE AT LEAST TALK ABOUT THE POLE?

GET OUT.

I DIDN'T SAY A THING.

I'M DONE ARGUING.

WHAT'S THE POINT?

BE MARRIED. HAVE FUN. ENJOY HER WHILE SHE'S HERE.

ENJOY ALL THE BEAUTIFUL, IF TEMPORARY, COMFORTS OF LOVE.

HAVE A BLOODY BALL!

LIVE THE DREAM.

"SOMETHING'S WRONG. WHAT'S WRONG?"

WE'VE SEEN AND SOLVED *THREE* FAIRLY VICIOUS MURDERS TONIGHT.

I HAD *CROC* WRAPPED AROUND ME AS I FELL FROM NEWTON TOWER.

AND, OF COURSE, *KITE MAN.*

THIS IS GOTHAM. *EVERYTHING'S* WRONG.

NO, THIS IS GOTHAM. EVERYTHING'S GOTHAM.

BUT *THIS* IS SOMETHING ELSE.

JUST TELL ME, BAT.

SO I CAN MAKE IT BETTER.

I...

SLAM

SCREEEEEE

YOU MIND HITTING *"ROOFTOP"* FOR ME, LOVE?

YOU CAN'T LIGHT THAT IN HERE.

WELL, GOOD THING THIS ISN'T A LIGHTER, IS IT?

AND THIS ISN'T A CIGARETTE, COME TO THINK.

AND THIS ISN'T MY MOUTH. AND THIS ISN'T AN ELEVATOR.

AND YOU'RE NOT A PERSON TALKING TO ME.

AND WE'RE NOT IN A BUILDING.

JUST SAYING...

DREAMS.

JUST 'CAUSE EVERYONE FOLLOWS YOU...

...YOU THINK YOU RUN THE BLOODY WORLD.

JOKER?

SNIPER...
IT WAS LIKE...
DICK...I...

THE
BEAST MAYBE.
AGAIN.

I DON'T
KNOW.

WHAT IS THIS?

THEY GOT YOU STRAPPED TO SOME MACHINE.

USING *SCARECROW* GAS TO INDUCE...THIS. ALL OF THIS.

WHATEVER CAME BEFORE, WHATEVER COMES NEXT.

THEY'RE TRYING TO DRIVE YOU BLEEDING MAD.

AH, NO, I'M SORRY, FRIEND. I'M HERE TO TELL YOU, YOU *CAN'T* GET OUT.

YOU'LL *NEVER* GET OUT. YOU WILL *GO MAD.*

NOT THAT YOU'LL REMEMBER IN THE NEXT ONE, BUT MAYBE...

NO, BATMAN, I'M NOT. NO ONE KNOWS YOU'RE HERE.

YOU'RE QUITE ALONE. I'M...

WELL, I'M JUST LIKE EVERYTHING ELSE AROUND HERE. JUST LIKE YOU, REALLY.

YOU'RE HERE TO HELP ME?

TO GET ME OUT?

YOU-- YOU'RE NOT JOHN.

DC COMICS PRESENTS

KNIGHTMARES, PART 3
"Smoke and Mirrors"

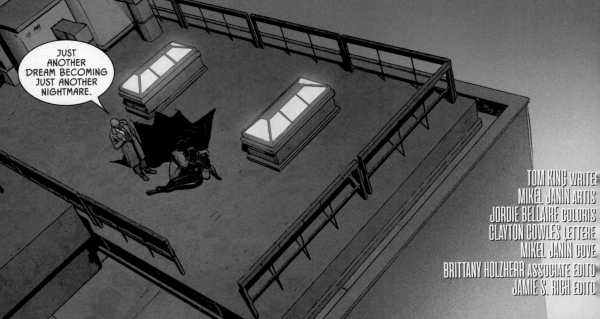

JUST ANOTHER DREAM BECOMING JUST ANOTHER NIGHTMARE.

TOM KING WRITE
MIKEL JANIN ARTIS
JORDIE BELLAIRE COLORIS
CLAYTON COWLES LETTERE
MIKEL JANIN COVE
BRITTANY HOLZHERR ASSOCIATE EDITO
JAMIE S. RICH EDITO

BATMAN
#66

CAN I HAVE ONE OF THOSE?

THANK YOU.

HE SENT YOU?

YOU DO EVERYTHING HE WANTS?

IN HIS DREAMS.

WE MET ON THE STREET.

"I LIKED THE WAY HE MOVED.

"I LIKED THE WAY HE TOUCHED ME.

"HE WANTED TO BE TOUGH--HE COULDN'T HELP BUT BE GENTLE.

"I LIKED HIS FACE."

"WELL. YOU HAVE TO UNDERSTAND.

"IT'D BEEN GOING FOR SOME TIME...

"...BEFORE IT BECAME SOMETHING NICE.

KKRSHHH

"BUT THERE WERE MOMENTS.

"LIKE THE MUSEUM."

"HE SAW ME. HE HESITATED.

"I LIKED THE SMELL OF HIM--LEATHER AND SWEAT.

"THEN HE GOT SHOT.

"HARVEY'D PAID ME 2,222,222 DOLLARS AND 22 CENTS FOR THE SETUP.

"PLUS I GOT TO KEEP THE DIAMOND."

"BUT, Y'KNOW, BAT WAS PREPARED.

"THAT BOY IS *ALWAYS* PREPARED.

"EXTRA ARMOR ON JUST FOR THE SHOT.

"SEE, THE WHOLE ROBBERY WASN'T WHAT IT WAS.

"IT WASN'T A WAY FOR HARVEY TO FIND BAT.

"*NO,* IT WAS A WAY FOR BAT TO FIND HARVEY.

"HARVEY'D COME TO ME, AND I'D GONE TO BAT.

"AND TOGETHER, WE DOUBLE-CROSSED TWO-FACE.

"WHICH, TO BE FAIR, HE OF ALL PEOPLE SHOULD'VE SEEN COMING."

"AFTER THAT IT BECAME FAIRLY REGULAR.
"NOW, I WASN'T *ALL* GOOD, HE WASN'T ANYTHING *BUT* GOOD.
"OR AT LEAST THAT'S WHAT WE TOLD OURSELVES AND OCCASIONALLY EACH OTHER.
"SO THERE WERE TENSIONS.
"BREAKS.
"I'D FIND SOMEONE ELSE, HE'D FIND WHOEVER.
"WE'D MAKE ALL THE BAD DECISIONS, BREAK ALL THE BEST HEARTS.
"AND IN THE END, THERE WE'D BE.
"SWEAT AND LEATHER.
"BAT AND CAT.
"I LIKED HOW HE HELD ME, LIKE HE COULD DO ANYTHING, BUT HE COULDN'T LET GO.
"SO WE'D ALWAYS COME BACK TO EACH OTHER."
FINGER ST.

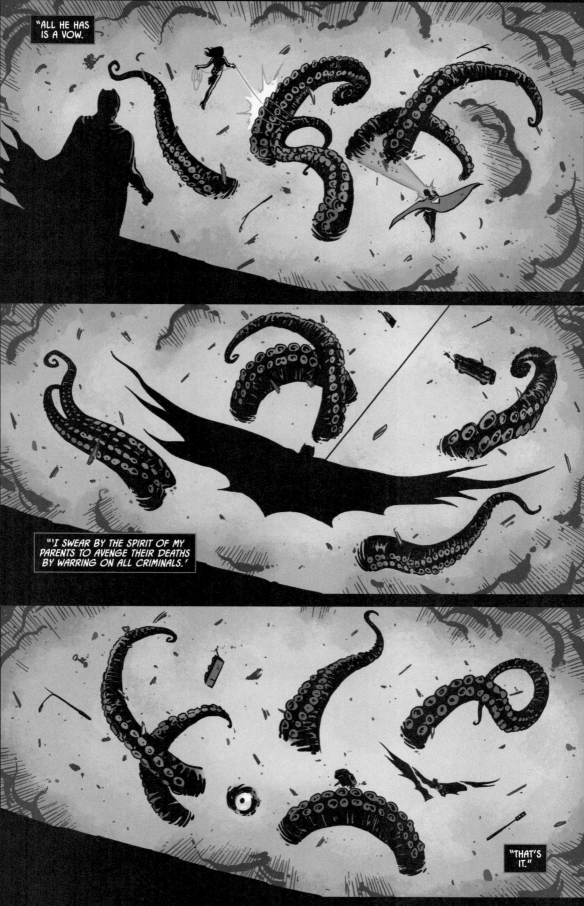

"I'M GOOD AT THIS GAME. THIS PUNCHING AND FIGHTING NONSENSE.

"GETTING ALL DRESSED UP FOR THE FIGHT.

"I BET YOU'RE PRETTY GOOD, TOO.

"THERE ARE LOTS OF US, AND LOTS OF US ARE GOOD AT IT.

"WE TRAIN OUR WHOLE LIVES, USE OUR TRAGIC BEGINNINGS AND OUR FORTUNATE ACCIDENTS.

"WE KICK, WE JUMP, WE FLY, WE SAVE THE DAY.

"BUT NONE OF US. NOT A ONE...

"...IS *HIM*.

"NO ONE ELSE IS...

"...*BATMAN.*"

"HOW? HOW DOES HE MAKE HIMSELF THAT GOOD?

"GOOD ENOUGH THAT WE CAN'T LIVE WITHOUT HIM?

"WITH JUST A VOW.

"HE TOLD ME ONCE. I WAS LOCKED UP. HE WROTE ME A NOTE.

"YOU SEE, IT'S NOT JUST A VOW.

"IT'S *ONLY* A VOW.

"AFTER HIS PARENTS, HE ABANDONED HIS LIFE AND EMBRACED THAT WAR.

"HE PUT IT ABOVE EVERYTHING.

"EVERY DOUBT, EVERY PAIN, EVERY INSTINCT OF RETREAT OR SURRENDER.

"EVERY LOVE."

SO HE CAN'T BE HAPPY *AND* BE BATMAN?

WHAT IS IT HE SAYS? YOU'VE HEARD HIM.

"I'M BATMAN BECAUSE I'M BATMAN."

HE CAN'T BE ANYTHING *AND* BE BATMAN.

I DON'T BELIEVE YOU.

OH, HONEY...

...DO YOU THINK I CARE?

WHY?

YEAH.

TWO GUYS WERE LOOKING AT A FLAG WAVING IN THE WIND. THEY WERE ARGUING.

ONE SAID THE WIND WAS MOVING, THE OTHER SAID THE FLAG WAS MOVING.

THEY CAN'T DECIDE SO THEY ASK THEIR BUDDY, AND THEIR BUDDY SAYS:

"YOU IDIOTS. DON'T YOU KNOW ANYTHING?"

"IT AIN'T THE FLAG. IT AIN'T THE WIND.

"IT'S YOUR MIND THAT'S MOVING."

YOU.

WHAT ARE *YOU* DOING HERE?

WHERE IS *HE?*

HE'S...TRAPPED. IN A SERIES OF NIGHTMARES.

THIS IS ONE OF THEM. *I'M* ONE OF THEM.

YOU'RE ONE OF THEM.

SO HE'S TRAPPED.

HE'S BATMAN.

HE'LL ESCAPE.

NO, YOU DON'T UNDERSTAND.

THIS *IS* HIS ESCAPE. ME. HERE. FINDING *THIS* TRUTH.

IT'S ALL HE CAN THINK TO DO.

WHAT? *YOU'RE* THE ANSWER?

NO.

I'M THE QUESTION.

KNIGHTMARES, PART 4
"Cat"

TOM KING WRITER JORGE FORNES ARTIST
DAVE STEWART COLORIST
CLAYTON COWLES LETTERER
MIKEL JANÍN COVER
BRITTANY HOLZHERR ASSOCIATE EDITOR
JAMIE S. RICH EDITOR

DC Comics PRESENTS

OKAY.

I LIED.

BATMAN
#67

DC COMICS PRESENTS

KNIGHTMARES, PART 5
"All the Way Down"

TOM KING WRITER
LEE WEEKS & JORGE FORNES ARTISTS

LOVERN KINDZIERSKI COLORIST
CLAYTON COWLES LETTERER
LEE WEEKS & ELIZABETH BREITWEISER COVER
BRITTANY HOLZHERR ASSOCIATE EDITOR
JAMIE S. RICH EDITOR

BEEPBEEP

BEEPBEEP

KKRSHH

FMMMMP

KKRSHH

CRRSHHH

BEEPBEEP

BEEPBEEP

C-C-C-C--

HE WENT THAT WAY.

RIGHT OUT THE FRONT DOOR.

SIR.

BATMAN
#68

THE SOUP IS GOOD.

YES. I AGREE.

IT'S. UH... YEAH. IT'S GOOD.

OH! THERE'S, UH... AN *ASTEROID*. HEADING TO EARTH. IT COULD, UH...

...*DESTROY* THE PLANET...

AH. WELL, IF YOU *MUST* GO...

DICK IS WATCHING THIS CITY. FOR ME. SO THAT WE COULD...

BUT I'M *SURE* HE COULD...USE *MY* HELP WITH THESE...RECENT TWO-FACE MURDERS...

WAIT, NO, NO, NO, IT'S FINE.

THERE'S *SUPERGIRL*. SHE'S GOT IT. IT'S HANDLED.

PROMISED YOU I'D BE HERE FOR YOUR... BACHELOR... *DINNER*, AND...UH...

I'M HERE.

YOU DID. PROMISE. RIGHT.

AND I... ALSO PROMISED. SO.

THANK YOU.

OF COURSE. MY PLEASURE. THANK *YOU*. I MEAN... UH...

LOOK AT THIS SOUP.

IT'S... REALLY GOOD.

YES. I AGREE.

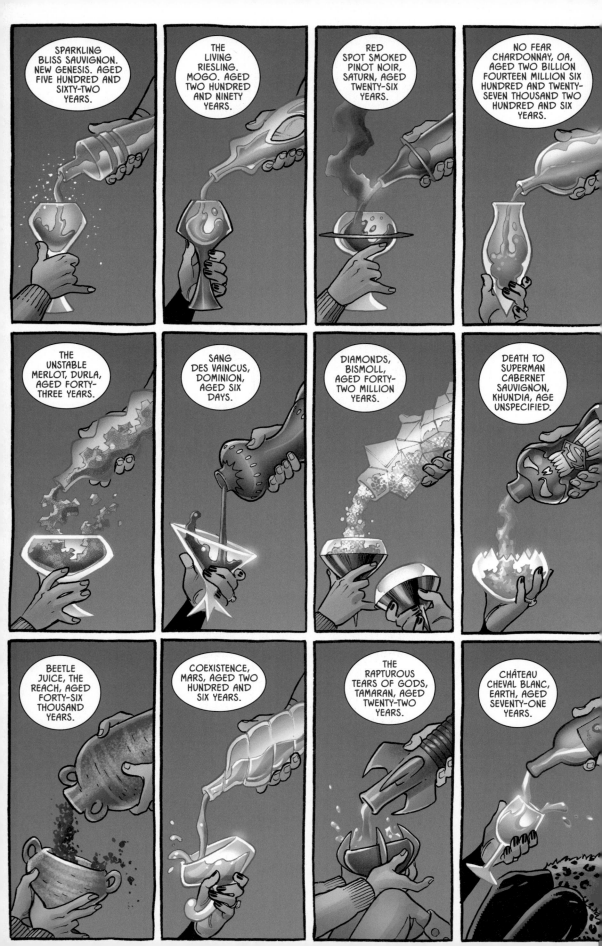

WHEN IT'S TOMORROW AND WE'RE SOBER, YOU REMEMBER...

...THIS WAS YOUR IDEA.

TOMORROW?

TOMORROW I HAVE TO WAKE UP AND BE A REPORTER AND A WIFE AND A MOTHER AND THEN GO TO WORK AND BE A REPORTER AND A WIFE AND A MOTHER AND THEN GO HOME AND BE A REPORTER AND A WIFE AND A MOTHER.

AND FOR ALL THAT. I GET...

ANOTHER TOMORROW.

RRRRRIPPP

$&$@ TOMORROW.

CHECK.

Y'KNOW, BRUCE, IF YOU **WANTED**, I COULD, UH...

IF YOU NEEDED **ADVICE** ON...MARRIAGE.

ANY **QUESTIONS** OR ANYTHING...

CHECK.

FRIEND TO FRIEND.

THIS IS A **BIG** STEP YOU'RE TAKING.

IF YOU WANT TO **TALK** ABOUT IT...

CHECK.

I FIND MARRIAGE QUITE REWARDING.

ACTUALLY.

I THINK IT MAKES A BETTER... UH, MAKES ME BETTER AT THIS JOB. **OUR** JOB.

CHECK.

I MEAN... I JUST WANTED TO ASK. IF **YOU** WANTED TO ASK.

'CAUSE IT'S GREAT.

AND I'M PROUD OF YOU, PAL.

MATE.

YOU DIDN'T NEED TO COME.

IT'S A LONG FLIGHT BACK. YOU MIGHT *DROP* HER.

I'VE CARRIED *THE GALAXIES* WITHOUT DROPPING THEM.

SHE'S MORE IMPORTANT THAN THE GALAXIES.

WE SHOULD DO THIS AGAIN.

WE *MUST* DO THIS AGAIN.

BATCAVE?

THERE'S, LIKE, A WHOLE *HUGE* VAULT FULL OF CONTRABAND...

YOU HAVE A GOOD TIME, LOIS?

ALWAYS.

CAT.

BAT.

HOW DID YOU GUYS DO? MANAGE NOT TO FIGHT ANY SUPER-ROBOTS?

NOPE, NO ROBOTS, WE PLAYED CHESS. IT WAS NICE.

I WON.

SURE YOU DID.

AND THE, *UH*... FORTRESS?

IT WAS *HER* IDEA.

IT WAS *NOT* MY IDEA!

I MADE A FRIEND.

YOU DID? GOOD. I...ENJOY FRIENDS.

ARE YOU MY FRIEND?

WELL...I... WE'RE GETTING MARRIED. I LOVE YOU.

"DEAR GOD,
BAT, I LOVE
YOU, TOO."

DC COMICS PRESENTS

KNIGHTMARES, PART 6

"Solitude"

TOM KING WRITER AMANDA CONNER, DAN PANOSIAN, JOHN TIMMS & MIKEL JANÍN ARTISTS

PAUL MOUNTS, JOHN TIMMS & JORDIE BELLAIRE COLORISTS CLAYTON COWLES LETTERER CONNER & MOUNTS COVER

BRITTANY HOLZHERR ASSOCIATE EDITOR JAMIE S. RICH EDITOR

BATMAN
#69

I DO ENJOY WATCHING YOU BLEED.

KKKKRKK

THOMAS... WAYNE.

A... SPOILED RICH... MAN...

WHO KNOWS... NOTHING... OF WHAT IT IS...

...TO BLEED.

NNN

I BROKE... BATMAN...

WHO ARE... YOU?

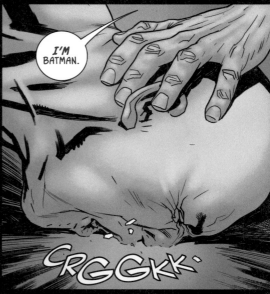

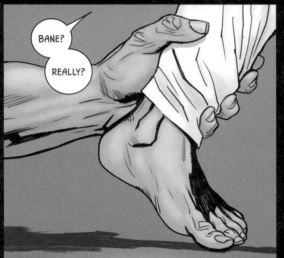

VARIANT COVER GALLERY

BATMAN #61 variant cover
by FRANCESCO MATTINA

BATMAN #62 variant cover
by FRANK MILLER and ALEX SINCLAIR

BATMAN #67 variant cover
by DAVE JOHNSON

BATMAN #68 variant cover
by FRANCESCO MATTINA

BATMAN #69 variant cover
by FRANCESCO MATTINA

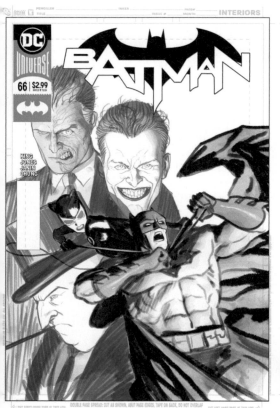

Unused cover concept sketches for **BATMAN #66** by MIKEL JANÍN

A.)

Unused cover concept sketches for **BATMAN #67** by LEE WEEKS

Rough pencils and final line art for **BATMAN #69** cover by YANICK PAQUETTE

THE #1 *NEW YORK TIMES* BESTSELLER
THE NEW 52!

BATMAN

VOLUME 1
THE COURT OF OWLS

"SNYDER MIGHT BE THE DEFINING BATMAN WRITER OF OUR GENERATION."
— COMPLEX MAGAZINE

SCOTT **SNYDER**   GREG **CAPULLO**   JONATHAN **GLAPION**

"[Writer Scott Snyder] pulls from the oldest aspects of the Batman myth, combines it with sinister-comic elements from the series' best period, and gives the whole thing terrific forward-spin."
– ENTERTAINMENT WEEKLY

START AT THE BEGINNING!
BATMAN
VOL. 1: THE COURT OF OWLS
SCOTT SNYDER with GREG CAPULLO

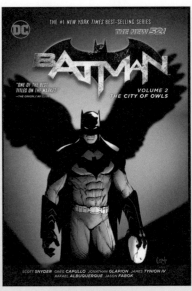

BATMAN VOL. 2:
THE CITY OF OWLS

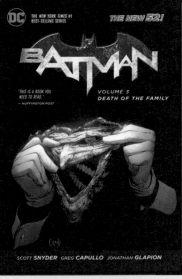

BATMAN VOL. 3:
DEATH OF THE FAMILY

READ THE ENTIRE EPIC

BATMAN VOL.
ZERO YEAR – SECRET CI

BATMAN VOL.
ZERO YEAR – DARK CI

BATMAN VOL.
GRAVEYARD SH

BATMAN VOL
ENDGAM

BATMAN VOL.
SUPERHEA

BATMAN VOL.
BLOO

BATMAN VOL.
EPILOG

Get more DC graphic novels wherever comics and books are sold!

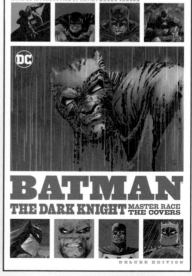

BATMAN
VOL. 1: I AM GOTHAM
TOM KING
DAVID FINCH

VOL. 1 I AM GOTHAM
TOM KING • DAVID FINCH

BATMAN: VOL. 2
I AM SUICIDE

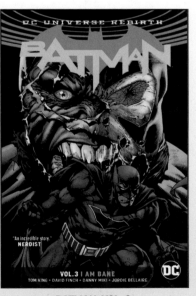

BATMAN: VOL. 3:
I AM BANE

READ THEM ALL

BATMAN VOL. 4: THE WAR OF JOKES AND RIDDLES

BATMAN VOL. 5: RULES OF ENGAGEMENT

BATMAN VOL. 6: BRIDE OR BURGLAR

Get more DC graphic novels wherever comics and books are sold!